Natural parks on the Canary Islands

EVEREST

Text: Francisco Javier Macías Martín

Photographs: Oliviero Daidola, Paolo Tiengo and Justino Díez

Layout: Gerardo Rodera

Cover design: Alfredo Anievas

Maps: © Everest

Translation: EURO:TEXT, Martin Gell

2nd EDITION
© EDITORIAL EVEREST, S.A.
Carretera León-La Coruña, km 5 - LEÓN
ISBN: 84-241-3572-5
Legal deposit: LE. 671-1998
Printed in Spain

EDITORIAL EVERGRÁFICAS, S.L.
Carretera León-La Coruña, km 5
LEON (Spain)

La Caldera de Taburiente National Park.

INTRODUCTION

The Canary Archipelago, situated in the Atlantic Ocean just off the northwestern coast of Africa, comprises seven main islands (Lanzarote, Fuerteventura, Gran Canaria, Tenerife, El Hierro, La Gomera and La Palma), as well as four islets (Alegranza, La Graciosa, Montaña Clara and Lobos) and an equal number of rocks soaring up from amidst the waves. According to data provided by the Spanish Institute of Statistics (INE), the islands have a total surface area of 7,501 km².

Due to their exceptional geographical position, the Canary Islands have always been a major nexus on the intercontinental sea routes linking Europe with America, Africa and Asia, a fact which has had a great bearing on many aspects of their history. The Canaries have belonged to the Spanish Crown since the 15th century and at present form an autonomous governmental region or *comunidad* subdivided into two constituent provinces, Santa Cruz de Tenerife (Tenerife, La Palma, La Gomera and El Hierro) and Las Palmas de Gran Canaria (Gran Canaria, Lanzarote and Fuerteventura).

There was a time when these islands were shrouded in legend. The ancient Greeks believed them to be a distant paradise and both Homer and Hesiod tell us of certain islands lying beyond the Pillars of Hercules (the Strait of Gibraltar), which they called the *Elysian Fields* and *Hesperides* and where life was easy and pleasant. Furthermore, this was to be the location chosen by Plato for the legendary island of Atlantis. The actual existence of the archipelago was to be recorded later on, in Roman times, Pliny the Elder himself referring to them in his writings as *Las Islas Afortunadas* or The Fortunate Isles, a sobriquet which is still used today.

Although many theories have been put forward regarding the origin of the Canary Islands, nowadays most experts agree on the volcanic nature of their genesis. In order to simplify matters, it can be said that the Canaries are a series of quite distinct volcanic structures that nevertheless bear a mutual relation. The concept of tectonic dynamics, or more specifically, that of continental drift, can explain the birth of these structures. Thirty million years ago, as it drifted eastwards, the African plate came to a sudden halt, giving rise to large cracks in the sea bed through which lava began to pour out. The accumulation of this volcanic material over many thousands of years gave shape to the islands we know today.

The National Parks of the Canary Islands feature a variety of landscapes and afford the visitor innumerable leisure possibilities. Left, Garajonay (La Gomera). Below, La Caldera de Taburiente (La Palma).

Las Cañadas del Teide.

Not far from the Canaries lie other groups of islands of similar characteristics regarding geology, climate, fauna and flora, namely the Azores, Cape Verde, Madeira and Ilhas Selvagens. Together they form an area of the Atlantic known as *Macaronesia*, a name derived from Greek words that curiously enough also mean "the fortunate isles".

The climate on the Canary Islands is of a clement nature, a fact which is owed amongst other things to their subtropical position close to the Tropic of Cancer. They lie at a latitude characterized by the predominance of a series of high pressures or anticyclones, above all that referred to as the Azores Anticyclone, which guarantee the prevalence of good weather. To this one must add the proximity of the African continent, which becomes particularly noticeable when the anticyclone withdraws to the north. On doing so, it brings on the Saharan winds, which frequently arrive laden with suspended particles of dust, thus giving rise to heatwaves. Whereas this type of weather is characteristic of the summer, in the winter the southward movement of the anticyclone brings cold fronts of polar origin to the islands, leading to heavy rainfall or even snow on the highest peaks.

View of the Dunas de Maspalomas Nature Reserve (Gran Canaria).

Garajonay. ▶

*Above, visitors at the Timanfaya National
Park (Lanzarote). Right, El Teide, true symbol of
Las Cañadas National Park (Tenerife).*

An equally important factor conditioning the
climate is the sea, which, in the form of the so-
called Canary cold current, helps to moderate what
would otherwise be far more extreme temperatures.
Also worthy of special note are the winds that often
sweep across the islands, the so-called Trade
Winds, whose true nature is revealed as they meet
the mountainous relief of the Canaries. The islands
act as a barrier impeding the circulation of these air
masses which, as they move across the Atlantic
Ocean, become moisture-laden. The geography of
the Canary Islands is characterized, among other
factors, by its sheer height. Almost without warning,
steep slopes are seen to rise abruptly from the coast
to the islands' peaks. Such are the obstacles
awaiting the Trade Winds as they make their way
up from more southerly latitudes. Thus forced to rise
sharply in a short space of time, the winds give rise
to the renowned *"seas of clouds"*, that is, the
condensation of the moisture they carry, most of
which is deposited on the islands' surface. This is
above all the case on the northern slopes of the
"high islands" - Tenerife, Gran Canaria, La Palma,
El Hierro and La Gomera -, so-called in contrast to
the "low islands", Lanzarote and Fuerteventura. The
latter, marked by the absence of any truly
mountainous terrain, are thus less favoured by the
above phenomenon, the singular importance of
which lies in the fact that it helps to maintain the
presence of water, the scarcest of the elements in
these parts.

It is important that we bear these peculiarities in mind, since they have led to the creation of the characteristic, unique ecosystems of the Canaries, some of which are truly without compare. It is true that the Canary Islands have lost a lot since the times when scientists such as Humboldt, Berthelot and so many others first described their geological, botanical and zoological features. Nevertheless, many of the latter still remain, and in order to protect them, a series of National Parks have arisen. At present there are four areas on the archipelago that enjoy this particular level of protection, namely Las Cañadas del Teide National Park on Tenerife, La Caldera de Taburiente National Park on La Palma, Timanfaya National Park on Lanzarote and Garajonay National Park on La Gomera.

The great variety of plantlife in the Canary Island National Parks is shown by these photographs taken at Garajonay (left), Maspalomas (below)...

Furthermore, the Canary Island Autonomous Government has deemed a series of other ecosystems - featuring a wide range of varying characteristics - to be worthy of a certain degree of protection. Together they form what is known as the Canary Island Network of Protected Natural Areas. Although each of the latter deserve to be included in this account, the scope of this book allows us to mention but two, both of which are situated on Gran Canaria: the Las Dunas de Maspalomas Special Nature Reserve and the El Nublo Rural Park and its surroundings. For some time now steps have been taken to provide this island with its own National Park, the exact geographical extension of which remains to be decided.

...La Caldera de Taburiente (right) and Las Cañadas del Teide (below).

TEIDE NATIONAL PARK

Tenerife is the largest of the Canary Islands
(2,057 km^2) and, like most of the others, it
features a rugged relief that is marked, amongst
other things, by a mountainous ridge stretching
across the island from the northeast to the
southwest. The crowning glory of Tenerife, the
Peak of El Teide, rises up from inside the Las
Cañadas volcanic caldera, that great circular
geological depression that forms the roof of the
island. An impressive volcanic cone, El Teide
soars to a height of 3,717 metres above sea level,
which makes it the highest mountain in Spain.
Declared a National Park on 22nd January 1954,
Las Cañadas del Teide has a surface area of 135
km^2 that extends into the districts of La Orotava,
Guía de Isora, Santiago de Teide and Icod de los
Vinos. The geological origin of the area has been
the subject of much debate amongst scientists.
According to Carracedo, El Teide and Las
Cañadas are the result of an episode of volcanic
activity that occurred about three million years
ago and which led to the creation of a great
dome standing between 3,000 and 5,000 metres
high. On the other hand, Martínez de Pisón and
Quirantes think more along the lines of the
formation of an irregular geological structure
dotted with valleys. Araña believes the process
involved several phases and an equal number of
eruptions. Nowadays, the prevailing theory is
that of the great dome, albeit in slightly varying
interpretations. Discrepancies still exist regarding
the origin of the Las Cañadas depression, that
enormous caldera encircling the peak and
marked by a great wall measuring 12 by 17 km.
The most favoured hypothesis is that
contemplating the collapse of the volcanic
dome.
Inside Las Cañadas, to the north of this 'natural
amphitheatre', we come across the geological
ensemble of El Teide-Pico Viejo which, similar in
appearance to a truncated cone, rises some
1,700 metres from its base. In reality, what we
have before us here is a mountain formed by the
eruption and subsequent superposition of several
volcanoes: Pico Viejo, Montaña Blanca, Pico
Cabras and Narices del Teide.

*The Peak of El Teide in the
Las Cañadas del Teide
National Park.*

The "Sea of Clouds" drifting over the Park.

Two views of snow-capped El Teide. ▶

Crowning the structure is the Pan de Azúcar or Pilón which, rising up from the depression called La Rambleta, still features fumaroles or steam vents, an unmistakable sign that the volcano remains active. Over the last few centuries there has been a succession of eruptions, the most important of which being that which came about in the late 18th century, giving shape to what we know today as Pico Viejo. The last time El Teide exploded was earlier this century, the eruption taking place at Narices del Teide on the western slope of the cone.

For many the true symbol of the Canary Islands, El Teide can be seen from most parts of the archipelago. This is especially the case in winter, when its snow-capped peak is a common sight, the snow occasionally extending down the mountainsides to cover the adjacent sections of Las Cañadas. At the foot of the mountain lies the Llano de Ucanca, an extensive plain bordered by the Roques de García to the north, by the limits of lava flows to the west and south, and by the wall of the Ucanca Summit to the east.

All over Las Cañadas, numerous solidified lava flows are to be found. Indeed, this is an area characterized by the so-called *malpaís* ('bad land') landscape, in which we can discover multi-coloured lava layers, in particular at Los Azulejos in the vicinity of the Parador Nacional.

Southern entrance to the Park.

Tackling the singular relief of the National Park.

Also to be seen next to these lava formations are volcanic bombs (globular lava masses) - some of which are very large -, *lapilli* (tiny volcanic fragments), and ash. Such then are the features of an environment whose boundaries are perfectly marked out to the south, east and west by high cliffs pierced by a series of valley-floors and *cañadas* or ravines that are known, logically enough, as Las Cañadas del Teide. Gradually, materials transported in the process of erosion have come to fill in these original channels, thus giving rise to more or less extensive plateaux. The *cañadas* were known to man way back in ancient times, when they were used by the native people of Tenerife, the Guanches, as routes for the transhumance or periodical transfer of their herds of animals. Indeed, the original inhabitants of Tenerife basically subsisted on livestock farming, so much so that the care of goats played a major role in the day-to-day existence of the various *menceyatos* or kingdoms into which the island was divided. Each of these political units governed over its own territory, although no such exclusive rights applied either to the mountain peaks or, oddly enough, to the areas of high mountains, including the Las Cañadas area itself, which was considered to be strips of common pastureland to which all farmers could take their herds in summer. This use of Las Cañadas has been confirmed by the discovery of numerous archaeological remains.

The cold season brings snow to the area. For the rest of the year, the Park landsape is characterized by the features of its high mountain climate.

The craggy landscape referred to locally as Los Roques. Above, Roques de García. Opposite, Roque Chinchado flanked by a large specimen of viper's bugloss. The signs of volcanic activity and the effects of erosion are to be found all over this area.

Furthermore, experts researching into the religion of the first settlers of the Canary Islands have revealed the meaning that the island mountains held for them. Basically, they embodied a Manichaean or dualistic conception of the universe featuring one deity of good - called either "Acorán", "Aborá", "Orahán", etc., depending on each specific island and its own individual interpretation - and another of evil, who in the case of Tenerife was called "Guayota" and was believed to reside inside "Echeide", that is, El Teide. The climate of the National Park shares the characteristics of that of high mountains, being conditioned, among other factors, by its altitude. Although it has an average temperature of around 9º C, temperatures are seen to vary widely from day-time to night. The insolation level is high and there is variable precipitation, although the latter varies in the course of the year. Winter features heavy rainfall combined with snow, which falls above all on the northern slopes of El Teide and can last for several months. This is not the case in Las Cañadas, however, where snow is present for a much shorter time.

The "Queen's Shoe".

Different views of Ucanca.

The harsh environmental conditions prevailing in the Park, the fluctuations in temperature and the factors of insolation and aridity, would lead us to believe that this were a landscape in which all interest lay in its geological make-up. Nothing could be farther removed from the truth. Amidst the remains of past volcanic episodes life is seen to prosper, a fact which is clearly demonstrated, above all in the spring months, by the extraordinary wealth of flora on display. The plantlife here is overwhelmingly Macaronesian in origin, although a number of species are in fact endemic to the area, some being so rare that it should come as no surprise that they caught the eye of botanical experts as early as the 18th century. The most noteworthy of these plants are the El Teide broom (Spartocytisus supranubius) and the laburnum (Adenocarpus viscosus), which, often appearing in perfect union, simply dominate the surroundings. The tangled stems of the broom are to be seen all around; somewhat lethargic in the harsh winter months, it flourishes magnificently in May. Rivalling the scent and colour of the broom is the yellow-flowered stunted laburnum.

On this and the preceding page: various examples of the geological formations in the Park.

The "Stone Rose" near the Park.

The El Teide daisy.

The El Teide blue viper's bugloss.

We should also draw the reader's attention to such plant species as the graceful, yellow-flowered *hierba pajonera* (Descourainia bourgeana); the pinkish *alhelí del Teide* (Erysimum scoparium), to be found amidst the lava flows; the unsophisticated Teide daisy, which no-one would ever suspect to be endemic to the Park; the El Guanche rose and several varieties of cistus. Neither should we overlook the red viper's bugloss or *taginaste rojo* (Echium wildprettii), an impressive example of Macaronesian flora that revels on the steep mountain sides, featuring slender leaves and soaring reddish-hued flowers that do full justice to its name. Belonging to the same family are the blue-flowered *taginaste azul* (Echium webbii) and the *taginaste picante* (Echium auberanium).

Preceding two-page spread: malpaís in Los Azulejos. A fine example of what can be termed the strange marriage of geology and plantlife.

The El Teide red viper's bugloss.

Way above, at a height of 3,000 metres and over, where the aforementioned species simply cannot survive, we find the emblematic variety of the Park, namely the Teide violet, considered by some to be the plant species that grows at the greatest altitude in Spain. Its outstanding feature is certainly not its size - at times it can scarcely be made out against the ground - but rather its scent and colour, which are truly unique during the time it is in bloom. Indeed, this is when the miracle of life is seen to pulsate all around, in sharp contrast to the aspect afforded by the Park in winter, characterized by skeletal shrubs bereft of flowers and occasionally, when conditions turn out to be extreme, even adorned with icicles. There are very few tree species characteristic of this region to be found in the area enclosed by the Park. In fact, we can mention but two: the Canary cedar, a tree which, featuring a twisted trunk, is perfectly adapted to the harsh conditions of these heights, and the Canary pine, a limited number of which prosper on the sheer faces of the caldera walls.

Vegetation in the Park and its surrounds.

Insects account for the greatest number and variety of fauna species to be found in the Park, over four hundred having been identified. As is the case with plants, animal life here has also developed certain particular features, even though its diversity is not quite as notable. Besides the insects, one must not overlook the *lagarto tizón* (Lacerta galloti), a black lizard whose habitat extends as far as some fairly high ground. Mammals are represented here basically by certain varieties of bat, the most remarkable of which is the one known as the "mountain bat". Completing the picture of animal life in the Park are its birds, amongst which we should mention the crow, the blue chaffinch, the great grey shrike, Koenig's partridge or *perdiz moruna* (Alectoris barbara

koenigi), the kestrel, the beautiful hoopoe, as well as rock doves. Neither should we forget the presence of certain introduced species such as the mouflon, which together with the omnipresent rabbit, is constantly subjected to the necessary controls.

The Park can be reached by road from various points of the island. Taking Santa Cruz de Tenerife as a reference, one possible route starts from the capital of the island and climbs to La Laguna and from there on to the town of El Rosario, at which point the road enters the Monte de Esperanza pinewood. In what is a constant ascent, we arrive first at Izaña and then at Portillo de la Villa. From here, and without leaving the car, we can cross the volcanic crater as far as Boca de Tauce.

Another recommended route starts from the tourist resort of Puerto de la Cruz in the north of Tenerife. We first head for La Orotava and from there we journey on through pines to Portillo de la Villa, right up amidst the mountain peaks. Yet another possible itinerary approaches the Park from the south, starting out from the tourist region encompassing Las Américas, Los Cristianos, El Médano and Reina Sofía Airport. This route climbs up to Vilaflor and then on to Boca de Tauce. These are the most frequently used routes to the Park, but there are many others - to find them, one need only consult a road map.

Mina de San José.

Northern lava formations.

Once in the Park, the visitor must follow the instructions displayed by the authorities. It is advisable to go first to to the Visitors' Centre, where one is supplied with all kinds of information, especially if one wishes to use the various paths that lead around the Park. At the disposal of visitors arriving at the park is a guide service, shelters, a picnic area, together with a Parador Nacional or state-run hotel open all year round and a cable-car lift that goes right up to the peak of El Teide, from where one can enjoy views of the other islands of the archipelago.

Izaña Astrophysical Observatory.

Cable-car.

Las Cañadas del Teide parador or state-run hotel, a good place to spend the night in the Park if one wishes to get to know it thoroughly.

Above, The Hermitage of Las Nieves. Below, Hiking in the Park is made easy by the provision of a series of well-signposted routes. Nevertheless, it is advisable to obtain information on the itineraries available before setting out.

LA CALDERA DE TABURIENTE NATIONAL PARK

Lying as it does almost at the very heart of the island of San Miguel de La Palma, La Caldera de Taburiente is nothing less than an enormous crater measuring nearly 10 km in diameter. Resembling a horseshoe in shape, it opens out to the southwest into Las Angustias ravine, its natural descent to the sea. It was given the name of "caldera" when the German geologist Leopold von Buch came to study the depression and arrived at the conclusion that it was the consequence of a great volcanic explosion. In his future studies, von Buch was to use this term to describe this and other basin-shaped openings of similar characteristics to be found scattered all over the planet. Today we know that the origin of this impressive geological formation was in fact quite different, being linked more to the effects produced by the agents of erosion, in particular water, than to any such explosive episode.

The second part of the Park's name, *Taburiente*, alludes to the island's prehistoric past. Certain experts on the language of the indigenous people of La Palma have translated the word as meaning "plain", although Taburiente was not in fact the name given to this area by the natives, coming as it did under the original kingdom or canton of *"Aceró"* (itself translated as "strong place" by some and as "crater" by others). When the Castilians arrived on La Palma in the late 15th century, the island was divided into several cantons, each one of which was governed by a king. *"Aceró"* was ruled by Tanausú, the last island *mencey* to be subjugated by the *conquistadores*.

Rocky crag, so characteristic of the Caldera de Taburiente landscape.

Information Centre at Roque de los Muchachos. *Park entrance at Los Brecitos.*

Chronicles inform us that this *Benahorite* king (a term derived from *Benahoare*, "My Land" or "The Place of My Ancestors", the name by which the original inhabitants of La Palma knew their land) took refuge with his followers inside La Caldera, where for some considerable time they managed to hold off the attack of the Spanish forces under the command of Alonso Fernández de Lugo. They were aided in their endeavours by the hostile geography of the area, the caldera itself only being accessible through a small number of passes, all of which were fiercely defended by the natives. Finally convinced of the futility of his efforts, the Castilian leader decided to resort to a ploy: he sent an emissary to the enemy, inviting the latter to talks. Tanausú accepted the offer and, escorted by many of his men, ventured out of La Caldera, upon which he was captured by his opponents. Most of the natives were enslaved, put on ships and sent to the Peninsula to be sold. They would not all make it to Spain, many preferring to die of starvation, including their leader who, as legend will have it, on leaving the shores of his island was heard to repeat over and over again the words: *"Vacaguaré"*, that is, "I want to die".

As far as the administration of La Caldera de Taburiente is concerned, it was declared a National Park in November 1954, becoming, after such highly renowned parks as Ordesa, Covadonga and El Teide, the fourth area to come under state protection and control. Having a total surface area of 57 km^2, 41 of which are actually taken up by La Caldera, the Park lies within the district of El Paso. However, at its perimeter there is a wide belt of land which, classified as a buffer zone and therefore also protected, extends into the neighbouring regions of Tijarafe, Puntagorda, Garafía, Barlovento, San Andrés y Sauces, Puntallana, Santa Cruz de La Palma and Breña Alta.

La Caldera and its Visitors' Centre at El Paso.

The "Sea of Clouds" moving across the Park. ▶

La Caldera is encircled by soaring, almost vertical walls that rise to a height of around 700 m, along with a series of equally high slopes graced with woods of the Canary pine. The common denominator of the geography of this area is its inhospitable nature, featuring as it does an abundance of sheer drops and massive crags, above all to the northeast, where it is bordered by the rock face called La Pared. The Park's altitude ranges from 400 metres in the basin interior to 2,426 metres at Roque de los Muchachos which, lying to the northwest, is its highest peak. There are also several other peaks surpassing 2,000 metres, such as El Cedro, El Pico de la Cruz and Roque Palmero. Rising up within the crater itself are a number of slender *pitons* or sharply pointed rocks such as the one at Idafe, an elevation that in prehistoric times was sacred to the indigenous peoples.

Two-page spread overleaf: a view of La Caldera de Taburiente. Pinewoods clearly dominate the scenery.

Characteristic features of the caldera walls are a series of strias and ravines, the latter forming an intricate network of passages that eventually wend their way into the *Barranco de Las Angustias,* a large ravine in which the water from all the others collects. It should be pointed out, however, that further up this ravine is the area of Dos Aguas, its first catchment basin. The whole area abounds in springs, sources, and streams, the water occasionally tumbling vertiginously down the sheer rocks, often giving rise to extraordinary waterfalls, such as that at Hoya Verde.

◀ *Roque de Idafe, the remains of an ancient volcano, held to be sacred by the original inhabitants of La Palma.*

Los Agujeritos.

La Caldera as seen from Cumbrecita.

Coastal mountainside near Roque de Los Muchachos and two views of the latter rocky formation.

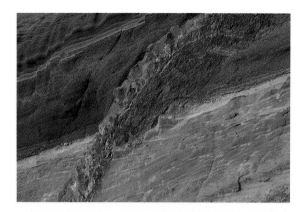

The constant presence of water and humidity in La Caldera has an influence on the plant and animal life there. The distribution of the vegetation is conditioned by the factors of altitude and, of course, geographical relief. In the most humid areas of the ravines there is an abundance of trees belonging to what is a unique botanical assemblage known as the Canary *laurisilva*, which as its name would suggest comprises members of the laurel family, such as the laurel itself (Laurus azorica or Laurus canariensis), the *viñátigo* (Persea indica), the *acebiño* or Canary holly (Ilex canariensis) and the *barbusano* (Apollonias barbujana). To be found growing alongside the *laurisilva* are a series of other plant species pertaining to a formation referred to here as *fayal-brezal* and basically featuring myrtle (*faya;* Myrica faya) and heather (*brezo;* Erica arborea). On the tall, jagged crags and the steeply rising rock faces we come across certain endemics that can be scientifically classified as rock flora. Example species are the rose-shaped *bejeque* (Aeonium spp.), with its large fleshy leaves; the *taginaste* or viper's bugloss (Echium spp.), the *tabaiba* or spurge (Euphorbia spp.) and the *verode* (Kleinia neriifolia).

Various geological aspects of the Park.

The Canary pine and plantlife in La Caldera de Taburiente.

Different plants are seen to appear as we move further up the mountain. Thus, the presence of laburnum becomes evident as from 2,000 metres, a height it shares with the La Palma violet, the broom (Spartocytisus supranubius) and the blue viper's bugloss (Echium webbii). Neither is it rare at such a height to see the twisted trunks of cedar trees gracing the scenery.

However, the aforementioned varieties alone do not suffice to explain the exuberant expanse of green dominating the Park's lanscape. The species responsible, one which we have referred to above as the great attraction of the islands, is the Canary pine. Indeed, pinewoods clearly predominate over any other kind of plant formation, and in this case are seen to include other botanical endemics that spring up in the shade of the pines, such as the *amagante* or cistus (Cistus symphytifolius) and the bright yellow-flowered *Gonospermum canariense*, known here as *faro* (or 'lighthouse', due to its beacon effect).

The Canary pine (*Pinus Canariensis*) is a variety specific to the archipelago. A large, sturdy tree, it has the peculiar characteristic of offering high resistance to fire - the result of its adaptation to an environment subject to frequent volcanic eruptions - and is thus able to regenerate and send forth new growth after being damaged by flames. This would seem to explain why considerable expanses of pinewoods remain on the peaks of islands such as La Palma, Tenerife, Gran Canaria, El Hierro and La Gomera.

The influence of man on the botanical varieties appearing in the Park surroundings is shown by the presence of certain species that have been introduced almost invariably to be used in agriculture or livestock farming.

Day-trippers at La Cumbrecita.

Such is the case of the fig and other fruit trees which are often seen to grow wild on once-farmed land that today lies abandoned. In other nearby areas - in particular on the slopes of the Las Angustias ravine, where the land is still worked today as a tribute to a time-honoured tradition - cereals, vines, tobacco plants and fruit trees have all appeared since La Caldera was declared a National Park. Amongst the species grown as feed for livestock are the *tedera* (Psoralea bituminosa), the *tagasaste* (Chamaecytisus palmensis) and the *haragán* (Ageratina adenophora).

As far as the Park fauna is concerned, there is a distinct lack of autochthonous vertebrates, since with the exception of a few reptiles such as the *perenquén* or gecko (Tarentola delalandii) and the *lagarto tizón* (Gallotia galloti palmae), one or other amphibian and some birds such as the rook, Boll's pigeon, the rock dove, the kestrel, the crow, the blackbird and the *capirote* (Sylvia atricapilla), most of the other animals did not in fact originate here. Exactly the same can be said of the mammals, a group dominated by goats and the species of mountain sheep called *arrui* (Ammotragus lervia). The latter, having been brought here a few decades ago for hunting purposes, has no natural predator and today has come to constitute a real menace to the farming areas close to the Park. Among the invertebrates the dominant group is that of the insects and if we were to choose a variety truly characteristic of La Caldera, then it would have to be either the *araña lobo* or wolf spider (Latrodectes spp.), which in spite of its size is totally harmless or the scolopendra - known here as the "centipede" - whose bite, whilst being very painful, is not in fact dangerous. Access to the interior of La Caldera can only be gained on foot, a fact which has greatly contributed to the conservation of its environment. A permit is needed, and this can be obtained from the Park offices located at the El Paso Visitors' Centre, where one is also supplied with all the necessary information on the routes to be followed. In all there are three entrance routes. The first of these starts from the *mirador* or vantage point at La Cumbrecita and wends its way down the Valle del Riachuelo; however, this route can be very dangerous, due not only to the ravines and high cliffs one encounters, but also to the frequent rockfalls, which occur especially in times of rain.

View of the El Roque de los Muchachos Astrophysical Observatory, situated in the spurs of La Caldera.
A waterfall, a truly common sight within the Park.

Water, the main attraction of the Park, along with its relief and plantlife.

The second route leads the visitor down the southern slope of the *Barranco de Las Angustias* along a track from Los Llanos de Aridane. Once at the foot of the ravine, one is faced by the journey up the course of the stream, a feat which is only really to be attempted in the dry season. It is not advisable to follow the stream in the wet season, since rainfall will lead to an unpredictable flow of water down the ravine, depending on the exact extent of the precipitation. In any event the best policy is to enquire about conditions before setting out. The third route, the most popular of the three, sets off from Los Brecitos which, lying on the northern wall of the Las Angustias ravine, is reached by at first following the same track mentioned in the second route, with the difference that instead of stopping at the ravine floor we continue, leaving the latter behind us and climb another extremely rugged track that leads us to Los Brecitos. From here, a perfectly signposted and well maintained path takes us inside La Caldera, where we find a well marked-out camping ground at the *Barranco de Dos Aguas*. This is where the crystal-clear waters of the streams flowing across Taburiente are seen to converge with those from Almendro Amargo, which owe their reddish hue to certain ferruginous contents. Around the rim of La Caldera we come across a large number of natural vantage-points, from which impressive views over the interior of the Park are to be enjoyed. Occasionally, however, the basin is shrouded by the renowned "sea of clouds", an equally curious phenomenon characteristic of the high-altitude islands of the archipelago. One of the most outstanding of these *miradores* is the one at Roques de los Muchachos, also the site of the Canary Island Astrophysical Observatory. Scientists from many countries come to work at this observatory, which at present ranks as one of the finest in the world.

GARAJONAY NATIONAL PARK

Situated on La Gomera, occupying the upper reaches of the island, this Park extends over an area of 3,948 hectares and features heights that range from 650 metres at its lowest point to 1,478 metres at the Garajonay peak. Having been declared a National Park in 1981, it was designated by UNESCO as part of the "Heritage of Mankind" in 1987. This is an area whose misty glades are steeped in legend. Even its name, Garajonay, is clearly redolent of the island's aboriginal past, referring as it does to a woeful tale of love between Jonay, a brave *Guanche* from neighbouring Tenerife who swam across the sea to La Gomera, and Gara, a beautiful Gomeran princess. According to tradition, Gara's family were bitterly opposed to the couple's union, as a result of which they had to flee into the heights of the island, where they hid in the dense woodland. However, they were soon found and, faced by the prospect of being separated, decided to leap together into the abyss from the highest peak of the island. Ever since, both the mountain and its woody surroundings have borne the name of the two lovers: Garajonay. Turning our attention now to less poetic matters, the National Park lies on an extensive plateau which, tilting slightly northwards, is situated in the island heights, almost at its very centre. This *meseta* is surrounded by precipitous terrain and is itself by no means lacking in lesser hills and valleys, some of which, such as that of El Cedro, feature a permanent stream of water. Such a panorama contrasts somewhat with the general geographical aspect of the island as a whole, the surface of which is furrowed with deep ravines or *barrancos* that bear witness to a long-lasting process of erosion. Moreover, the appearance of La Gomera was not altered by the Quaternary volcanic activity that so greatly affected the rest of the archipelago. Thus, the deep *barrancos* of the island are seen to originate on the edges of the central plateau and run radially in all directions. Looking once again at the Park itself, we should point out that although gently undulating contours are indeed predominant, this does not imply a complete absence of sharply contrasting features, which are to be seen in the shape of tall, pointed rocks or *pitons* and sheer rock faces. The latter stand at the edges of the plateau, whereas the former signal the site of ancient eroded volcanoes, of which all that remains today are their solidified vents, and are scattered all over the protected

region, even though they predominate in the eastern section. The rocks have been given such impressive names as La Mula, Ojila, Zarcita or Ogando, the latter being the most outstanding example. Another specimen, Cherilepí, presides over its surroundings at the centre of the Park.

Garajonay National Park boasts a diverse, luxuriant vegetation that has on occasions been compared to that of a humid tropical forest and which, featuring moss and lichens both on the ground and on the tree-trunks, is shrouded in cloud most of the year.

One of the entrances to the Garajonay National Park.

Two-page spread overleaf: a view of the Park. ▶

Park entrance at Carboneras, in the Chejelipes area.

The Park scenery is dominated by the *laurisilva* woodland which, covering over 2,500 hectares, includes as its main varieties the laurel (Laurus canariensis), the *barbusano* (Apollonias barbujana), the *til* (Ocotea foetens) and the *viñátigo* (Persea indica), alongside which a great number of other trees and shrubs are seen to prosper. Together, they constitute a unique formation, a true relic of a distant past, transporting us back to the Tertiary, to a time when large expanses of North Africa and Southern Europe were covered by a similar vegetation. The creation of the Garajonay National Park came precisely in response to the need to provide an efficient means of preservation for this singular flora, which extends primarily over the northern and northeastern sections of the protected area, above all in the regions of Los Acebiños, Mériga and El Cedro.

The characteristic "Sea of Clouds".   *View of the Park featuring Roque Cano, seen from Mount Tobares.*

A partial view of the Park including the road that wends its way through it. The "Chipude Fortress".

Appearing alongside the *laurisilva* is another Canary formation, the so-called *fayal-brezal*, featuring aromatic evergreen myrtle or *faya* (Myrica faya) and heather or *brezo* (Erica arborea). This is to be found principally in the eastern and southern sections of the Park, where the development of the *laurisilva* has either been affected by insolation levels or even halted by the activities of man. In the southern sector of the Park we also find the Canary pine (Pinus canariensis) sharing its environment with other recently introduced species such as the Monterey pine (Pinus radiata) and the eucalyptus.

Rocky crags of volcanic origin at Hermigua, exemplifying the rugged relief of La Gomera.

View of the Park, with the Garbato reservoir.

Rock formations in the Park.

Roque de Agando. ▶

The nature of the Park as a whole is defined by the combination of its geographical features, its climate and vegetation. Reaching La Gomera laden with moisture, the Trade Winds are forced to rise quickly over a short period of time, in such a way that when they come to the island heights, the area occupied by the Park plateau, the famous 'sea of clouds' is formed, densely encircling the rich vegetation. The moisture is then trapped by the branches of the various plant species present, in particular those belonging to the *laurisilva*, and on condensating it drips to the ground, thus bringing life to the surroundings. The woodland on La Gomera, as is the case with other islands characterized by high altitudes, provides a guaranteed supply of water, such a scarce commodity in this part of the world. The presence of water on the island is also to be attributed to its numerous permanent springs and its streams, the most important and fastest flowing of which being that which passes through El Cedro.

The Visitors' Centre (above) featuring a reconstruction of a peasant's dwelling (below).

The Park's laurisilva woodland. ▶

Spurge.

Heather.

Laurel.

The laurisilva woodland, a natural relic from the Tertiary.

The outstanding feature of the local fauna, and indeed that of the rest of the archipelago, is its rich variety of insects. Vertebrates are present here in the form of small mammals such as rabbits, black rats and bats. The most noteworthy of the birds on view in the Park are its three varieties of pigeons and doves, namely the *paloma rabiche* (Columba junoniae), the *paloma turqué* (Columba livia canariensis) and the rock dove (Columba livia); whereas the first variety nests in rocky areas, the second prefers woodland and the third normally chooses coastal cliffs. Among the other birds to be seen are wild canaries, chaffinches and blackbirds.

Travelling by road from the capital of La Gomera, San Sebastián, the Park can be reached via Arure, located right up in the mountains. From here, roads lead off to El Rejo, Juego de Bolas and Agulo and this is also where others from Vallehermoso, Alajeró and El Cercado converge.

As in the rest of the archipelago, insects are seen to dominate the Garajonay fauna. A butterfly.   *Sweet spurge.*

Above left, the myrtle-heather formation and pines in southern Garajonay.

Above right, a recreational area at Laguna Grande.

The Garajonay Visitors' Centre situated at Juego de Bolas supplies all the necessary information on the Park and offers for sale a selection of maps, brochures, videos, and similar items. Leading the visitor around the park are a series of well marked and not overdemanding paths that afford a variety of views of this most privileged setting. A guide service is available free of charge upon request from the relevant offices.

Below, the Hermitage of Nuestra Señora de Lourdes at El Bosque del Cedro.

TIMANFAYA NATIONAL PARK

Situated on Lanzarote, the easternmost of the
Canary Islands, Timanfaya was declared a
National Park in 1974. Featuring a surface area
of around 5,198 hectares, it lies within the
districts of Yaiza and Tinajo and is an area
primarily characterized by volcanic activity in its
many and varied forms. The truth is that
Timanfaya is one great volcanic lava field, the
result of a series of eruptions that occurred from
1730 to 1736 and another subsequent explosion
in 1824. Historical records clearly show that the
whole area was formerly of great agricultural
importance, producing as it did vast amounts of
cereals, which not only provided food for the
island, but were also exported to the rest of the
archipelago. However, throughout the above-
mentioned period of time (1730-1736) there was
a succession of volcanic explosions along the
Timanfaya massif in the west of the island,
releasing gas into the atmosphere and covering
the area with volcanic ash and lava. The
appearance of these once luxuriant fertile lands
was completely transformed, turning them into
an inhospitable, desolate landscape that spread
out over about 20,000 hectares.

There followed a period of calm which lasted
until well into the 19th century. But then,
between July and October 1834, the bowels of
the earth seemed to shake once more, although
less violently than in the previous episode. Fresh
craters appeared on the land that had already felt
the full effect of volcanic action.

The present-day Park extends precisely over the
part of the island where past volcanic activity has
left its deepest mark. Here, one is overwhelmed
by the presence of rock, dominating as it does
the entire scenery. The rock itself displays a
limited range of colours, dark, ochre, reddish
and yellowish hues being the most common. All
around volcanic cones rise into the air amidst
accumulations of lapilli, bombs, ash and the
crust of huge lava flows, some of which, forming
an almost flat surface, spread right out to the
horizon, where they disappear from sight. Indeed
it would seem that we were standing on another
planet, or that this was Earth as it was millions of
years ago. The Timanfaya National Park was thus
created in order to protect what is a quite unique
geological formation.

Entrance to the National Park.

Preceding two-page spread and above: visitors to the Park often choose to travel by camel.

Although at first sight the name Timanfaya would seem to be nothing more than a synonym for 'volcano', the truth of its origin is in fact rather more complex. As was the case with the other National Parks described above, in order to fully comprehend the meaning of Timanfaya, it is necessary to refer to the island's aboriginal past and to its legends. According to tradition, way back in the late 14th century a Spanish vessel under the command of Biscayan Martín Ruiz de Avendaño was driven by a storm to the shores of Lanzarote. Zonzamas, the king of the island, received the Spaniards with great hospitality. Those islanders best versed in such legendary tales also tell of the love that flourished between the noble seafarer from the Peninsula and Faina, the king's wife and how it came to pass that nine months after the former had parted, the queen gave birth to a light-skinned baby girl whom she named Ico. When Zonzamas died he was succeeded by his son Tiguafaya, also called *Timanfaya*, whose reign was destined to be a short one, since it would not be long before several Castilian slave ships arrived on the island. Many natives were captured, including Timanfaya himself, who was never again to return to his homeland. Subsequently, Guanareme, brother of the ill-fated king, came to the throne and made Ico his queen. The fruit of their union was Guadarfía, who was king of Lanzarote when the *conquistadores* arrived in 1402.

Lava landscape in the Park. ▶

Visitors are shown natural phenomena at Islote de Hilario. The extremely high underground temperatures reveal that all volcanic activity has not yet ceased.

The heat from inside the Earth is used for cooking.

Another good way to see the Park is on board a "guagua" or coach.

The Park landscape.

These photographs display the predominant relief of the Timanfaya National Park.

It would seem that we were on another planet...

Park scenery.

Blinded by the extraordinary geological features of the Timanfaya area, it would be all too easy for us to overlook its biological aspect, the life it holds. Certainly the characteristics of the land here are by no means ideal for either flora or fauna, but it is no less true that nature, in its immense wisdom, has created life forms capable of adapting to even the most extreme environmental conditions. Timanfaya was to prove to be no exception, even though in addition to the limitations of the soil, the local climatic conditions are extremely harsh, owing to the absence of any great heights and the proximity of the African continent. Nevertheless, the presence of the sea nearby does help to alleviate somewhat the extreme heat and the dryness of the atmosphere (annual rainfall figures stand at under 100 mm).

The first forms of plantlife to colonize this environment were lichens, and today these associations of algae and fungi remain the most commonly found, hundreds of species having been recorded. Predominant amongst the lichens are the so-called xerophytic plants, that is, those species which are perfectly adapted to dry climates, over a hundred and fifty having been identified to date. Lichens are normally seen to grow in areas in which the oldest geological formations prevail, referred to here as *"islotes"*, that is, "islands" of terrain untouched by lava flows. Examples of this are found at Islote de Hilario, Montaña de los Halcones, Montaña de

Inside the Park: the view form the road.

Tremesana and El Chinero.
Varieties of flora noteworthy for their peculiarity to this area are the yellow-flowered *tojío* (Odontospermum intermedium), the bluish-flowered *lengua de vaca*, and a smaller woody specimen with light-coloured leaves known as *salado blanco* (Polycarpea robusta). All of these species are in fact deemed to be endemic to Lanzarote. Several Canary Island endemics are also represented here, such as rosemary, perforate St. John's wort, *ratonera* (Forsskaolea angustifolia) and *verode* (Kleinia neriifolia), as well as two varieties - wild and sweet - of spurge (Euphorbia spp.) and *aulaga majorera* (Launaea arborescens).

View from Islote de Hilario out towards Montaña Rajada.
Unbelievable as it may seem, plants spring up from amidst the lava.

One of the stages of the "Volcano Route".   *Timanfaya.*

*Two views
of Timanfaya.*

Amidst the lava and other volcanic materials a singular plantlife is seen to grow, one which has managed to adapt to such an inhospitable environment as this.

Timanfaya, as seen from Yaiza.

Another highlight of this habitat is the presence of rushes, not because they often grow to a height of two metres, but rather because this is a plant type more characteristic of wetlands. Nevertheless, here we see them, scattered across the slopes of the volcanic cones, above all on those sections caressed by the sea breeze. Experts agree that the existence of rushes here can only be explained by their very situation, part of the ocean winds' humidity being deposited amongst the porous rocks covering this area, thus maintaining a level of moisture sufficient to enable these plants to survive. As far as the Timanfaya fauna is concerned, once more insects are seen to far outnumber all other groups. The rich variety of invertebrates present is displayed by the number of species recorded, some 120, a large percentage of which choose to flee from the high daytime insolation and are totally nocturnal in their habits. Such is the case of the local beetles and grasshoppers. The amount of vertebrates present is much more limited. One or other reptile is to be found, notably the peculiar *lagarto de Haría* (Gallotia atlantica), a small lizard perfectly adapted to the surroundings. Amongst the birds gracing the Park are the rock dove, the turtledove, the swift, the crow, the *guirre* or Egyptian vulture (Neophron percnopterus) and above all, the *pardela cenicienta* or Cory's shearwater (Calonectris diomedea). Access to the Timanfaya National Park poses no great problem and the routes leading there are easily followed by referring to any of the most widely available guidebooks. Nevertheless, we would recommend the visitor approach the area from either Yaiza or Tinajo. The Park has its own Information Centre, which will answer all enquiries regarding proposed visits.

Vineyards on the outskirts of the Park.

Mancha Blanca Visitors' Centre.

Yaiza, as seen from the Park.

Amongst the many alternatives open to visitors on arriving at the Park is that of boarding a *guagua* (the Canary Islanders' word for bus) and setting off on a 14-km ride along the so-called *Ruta de los Volcanes* or Volcano Route. Departing from Islote de Hilario, the tour passes El Manto de la Virgen and takes in the *mirador* at Montaña Rajada, a vantage-point commanding views over practically the entire Park. Continuing on along the Barranco del Fuego and the Valle de la Tranquilidad, the route climbs the Timanfaya mountains to then take a different way back to the departure point at Islote de Hilario. The trip affords one the unique experience of travelling through what is a truly extraordinary landscape, the expression of subterranean volcanic activity that has not yet concluded, as is witnessed by the so-called *hornillos* or little furnaces, holes dug into the surface in which dry branches will spontaneously burst into flames and from which jets of steam will shoot out as soon as any water is poured inside.

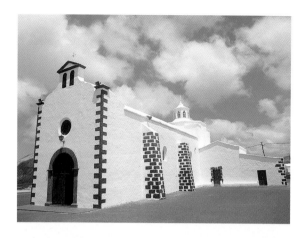

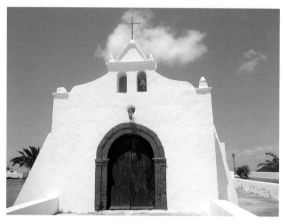

The area surrounding the Park.
Above top, the Hermitage of Los Dolores at Mancha
Blanca. Above bottom, Tiagua Hermitage. Opposite,
La Gería.
Below, Tiagua Agricultural Museum.

GRAN CANARIA

"LAS DUNAS DE MASPALOMAS" SPECIAL NATURE RESERVE

This nature reserve is situated in San Bartolomé district in southern Gran Canaria, near to the point where the Fataga, Ayaguares and Camoriscán ravine streams flow out into the sea, and a stone's throw away from the area's famous tourist resort, *Playa del Inglés.* This is an area dominated by expanses of dunes comprising minute phonolitic grains which are tossed around playfully by the ever-present wind. Such sandy formations bear witness to geological activity that occurred in the distant past, at a time when this area was still covered by the Atlantic Ocean, a fact that is demonstrated by the large number of stone remains to be found on higher ground. The Quaternary period featured a series of climatic changes which led to the dispersal of the waters, thus giving rise to a low coastal landscape marked by an abundance of the products of erosion. The dunes are a dynamic phenomenon that never seem to come to rest. The wind causes the sands to shift and with them, the dunes themselves.

The overwhelming sensation afforded by this area is one of aridity. However, what we have before us here is a habitat characterized by the presence of a plantlife that is perfectly adapted to its surroundings. Amongst the most notable species to be found here we should highlight the Canary tamarisk, the palm trees, the rushes and the *salado* (Schizogyne glaberrima), although a number of others are also present, such as the *balancón* (Traganum moquini) and the *juncia* (Cyperus laevigatus).

The dunes of Maspalomas, such fanciful forms sculpted by the winds.

The vegetation itself contributes to the formation of the dunes.

Strong, healthy palm trees rise up above the otherwise impoverished plantlife.

Vegetation characteristic of alluvial plains.

Above and opposite, La Charca de Maspalomas, a true jewel of the local environment which today is showing clear signs of recovery.

Life in La Charca: 1) Dragonfly (Gallinula chloropus); 2) Moorhen; 3) Duck; 4) Lizard.

Lying within the limits of the area declared Special Nature Reserve we come across the *Charca de Maspalomas,* a marsh whose rich variety of plant and animal life was once marvelled at by such naturalists as Bannerman, Bolle and Thaner. Indeed, in the late nineteenth century, these wetlands featured an abundance of sea birds and a flourishing, highly adapted vegetation. In the course of time, the human impact on this environment has increased and a look at the area today reveals how the combination of urban development and mass tourism has gradually depleted the former variety of life forms. The latter is now limited to a predominant species of reed (Phragmites australis) and some algae. As far as the local fauna is concerned, the most noteworthy species to be found are the starling, the moorhen and the coot. All in all, they constitute a pale reminder of what in the past was a myriad of life forms. Fortunately, the great concern that has arisen in recent years regarding the preservation of this environment has led the island authorities to

take considerable steps to ensure that it is properly cared for, so much so that at present we are beginning to witness the regeneration of what is a truly unique area.

El Roque Nublo, with El Teide in the background. Two of the great symbols of the Canary Islands. ▶

The northern edge of the peaks, on the way down to Valleseco. The town of Tejeda and Roque Bentaiga. ▶ Two-page spread overleaf: El Nublo, as seen from Los Pechos. In the background, Tenerife. In the foreground, the pinewood.

EL NUBLO RURAL PARK

Declared a Rural Park by the Canary Government in 1987, El Nublo forms part of the Natural Parks of Ojeda, Inagua y Pajonales and Tejeda, constitutes the most outstanding section of the Natural Park of the Southwestern Massif, and furthermore covers a small part of the Natural Park of Ayaguares y Pilancones. The Park was awarded its present-day status as a result of the 1994 Canary Islands' Natural Spaces Act. Spreading out over central and southwestern Gran Canaria, the Park runs along the Tejeda basin, the Sándara mountains and the southwestern *barrancos* or ravine streams that wend their way down to the coastal cliffs. The focal point of the Park is the La Cumbre massif which, commanding as it does the central area of the island, rises to its highest point at the peak of Las Nieves (1,965 m), although one should not overlook Los Pechos (1,951 m) or Roque Saucillo (1,850 m). The protected area accounts for approximately 26,307.4 hectares and encompasses land belonging to several island districts, above all those of Tejeda, Artenara, San Nicolás de Tolentino, Mogán, San Bartolomé, San Mateo, Valleseco and Moya. High on the list of the factors that were deemed to justify the decision to protect this environment were the variety of its habitats, the presence of endangered endemics such as the *rosalillo* (Dendriopoterrium pulidoi), a palm-like burnet of the rose family and the existence of large pinewoods, man-made marshes and cliff-lined coasts.

Such expanses of woodland help to shield the soil against erosion and also do much to replenish the supply of underground waters.

The area's geography is characterized by a variety of volcanic materials and a series of rugged contours, the result of several centuries of erosion. Lying amidst these geographical features is the Caldera de Tejeda, a strikingly spectacular crater whose origin is linked to the collapse of an ancient geological structure, the resulting depression itself having collapsed as a result of subsequent eruptions.

It is within the limits of the Park that we come across the oldest geological material to be found on Gran Canaria. Rising up amidst the rugged scenery at the centre of the island is Roque Nublo, an outstanding 60 m-high rocky peak, a vestige of volcanic activity dating from the Miocene and the Pliocene eras. It is flanked by a series of other enormous rocks of identical origin such as the Roque de Bentayga, itself a place once held to be sacred by the native people of Gran Canaria. One of the final episodes of the Castilian conquest of Gran Canaria was to take place on El Nublo, when the island chief Bentejuí, preferring to perish rather than surrender to the invaders, plunged to his death from the peak. El Nublo is doubtless to be considered the true symbol of Gran Canaria, which should come as no surprise since the original inhabitants of the island, the Canaries, also deemed this peak to be sacred. The island authorities have taken great pains to ensure the protection of El Nublo and its surroundings and have declared it a Natural Monument.

Los Llanos recreational area.

Looking out to Ayacata from the foot of El Nublo.   *Los Pechos, seen from El Nublo.*

The decision to elevate the peak to this new status was in part founded on the need to preserve such an ancient geological structure which in times gone by marked the heart of the island. Logically, the fact that the El Nublo area is of such symbolic value to the people of Gran Canaria also had a great bearing on the matter. The climate of the Park is seen to vary from one altitude or geographical context to another. The temperatures recorded at the peaks depend on the exact orientation of the land; thus, those areas facing north register considerably lower values in winter and often feature night frost and snowfalls. Summers are marked by more moderate temperatures. On the southern slopes, winters are milder and the summers hotter. The major form of plantlife seen to dominate these highlands is the pinewood, appearing as it does just a little way down the mountainside from the areas featuring high mountain xerophylous speices. Here, the pinewood comprises two main species, namely, the Canary and the Monterey pines. In the past the unbridled exploitation of these woods almost led to their complete destruction, and over the last few years efforts have been made to repair the damage done by encouraging reforestation programmes featuring the said two species. The best preserved pinewoods of Gran Canaria, stretching out over an area of more than 3,920 hectares, are to be found within the Inagua Comprehensive Nature Reserve, itself lying in an area of the Rural Park bordered by the villages of Mogán, Tejeda and San Nicolás. Consequently, and as a result of the fact that several ravine streams have their sources here, this area plays a vital role in the conservation of the island's water supplies. As we progress further down the mountainside, we find that the Canary pine is replaced by other plants. In certain areas its place is taken by the palm, the *acebuche* (Olea europaea), the *sabina* or juniper and the Canary cedar. In other parts - those whose evolution has been conditioned by man - the predominant species are the *retama* (Teline microphylla), the *escobón* (Chamecytisus proliferus), the *aulaga* (Launea arborescens), the *leña buena* (Neochamalaea pulverulenta), the *tabaiba amarga* (Euphorbia obtusifolia) and the *balo* (Plocarna pendula). Also putting in an appearance in these areas is the dragon tree, a mythical legendary tree endemic to the Canary Islands. The lowest lying stretches of land are occupied by the Canary spurge and other varieties of spurge.

The rocky crags at Tirajana. ▶

Pinewood at Tamadaba.

Right, from top to bottom: cave-dwelling at Acusa; Los Hornos dam; El Mulato dam.

Opposite page: vegetation at Ayacata.

Last page: various views of the Park.

Among the species belonging to the animal kingdom that are to be found in the Park are birds such as the *picapinos* or great spotted woodpecker, the blue finches - seen above all in the pinewoods - as well as the blue tit and the red-legged partridge. As far as reptiles are concerned, we should point out the presence of the three-toed skink, whereas among the mammals, the rabbit is by far the most predominant species.

Most of the area that goes to make up this Rural Park is considerably marked by human activity, a fact borne witness to not only by the presence of various villages, but also by that of farms devoted both to agricultural produce and livestock breeding. A further sign is of course the local road network. Of the many beautiful spots gracing this environment we should highlight Cruz de Tejeda, where we come across a vantage point from which we can enjoy marvellous views; and the equally impressive *miradores* at La Cuevita in Artenara and at La Culata, the latter being located on the road from Cruz de Tejeda to Cueva Grande. For those readers in search of peace and quiet, we suggest a visit to the recreational areas situated on the perimeter of the Park, such as those of Morro de Santiago, Llano de la Pez and Cueva de las Niñas.